D0442912

— THE GOURMET KITCHEN —

MUSHROOMS

WRITTEN BY JACQUELINE CLARK
ILLUSTRATED BY LINDA SMITH

SUNSET PUBLISHING CORPORATION

MENLO PARK, CALIFORNIA

A QUARTO BOOK

Copyright © 1994 Quarto Inc.
First edition. World rights reserved. No part of this publication may be reproduced by any
mechanical, photographic, or electronic process, or in the form of a phonographic recording,
nor may it be stored in a retrieval system, transmitted, or otherwise copied for public or private
use without prior written permission from the publisher.

Library of Congress Catalog Card Number: 94-66124

ISBN 0-376-02758-4

This book was designed and produced by
Quarto Inc.
The Old Brewery, 6 Blundell Street
London N7 9BH

Editors: Kate Kirby, Laura Washburn, Susan Ward
Art Editor: Mark Stevens
Designer: Julie Francis
Art Director: Moira Clinch
Editorial Director: Sophie Collins

First published in North America in 1994 by Sunset Publishing Corporation
Menlo Park, CA 94025

First Sunset printing September 1994

Typeset in Great Britain by West End Studios, Eastbourne, UK
Manufactured in Hong Kong by Regent Publishing Services Ltd.
Printed in China by Leefung-Asco Printers Ltd.

Contents

INTRODUCTION 4

STARTERS 12

MAIN DISHES 27

SIDE DISHES 48

ACCOMPANIMENTS 55

INDEX 64

INTRODUCTION

*W*ild mushrooms are one of the most delicious foods that Mother Earth provides. Finding these unlovely treasures, however, is the trick. Mushroom hunting takes place in the Autumn and, to a lesser degree, in the Spring, when experts visit the woods, forests, and fields to discover what may be growing there. The mushrooms' favorite habitat is damp, dark, and leafy, so an experienced, trained eye is needed to spot them hiding in the undergrowth.

Mushrooms can be found all over the world — some countries are just more aware of their culinary value. In France, as in the rest of Europe, mushroom hunting is a national pastime, and most people have quite a wide knowledge of the different varieties. There, if a species is unknown, the local pharmacist will identify it, and mushroom charts are often to be seen in the drugstore window during the Autumn months.

Unfortunately, neither this service, nor such prominently displayed charts, exist here, so beware of fungi which are unidentifiable — they could be poisonous. Do not attempt to hunt and eat any mushrooms unless their identities are confirmed by a mycologist, a botanist who specializes in fungi.

TYPES OF MUSHROOMS

Mushrooms are either cultivated or wild. Most of the varieties included in the following recipes are now cultivated. However, the more common types of wild ones are also listed because they can be bought fresh or dried at specialty groceries and delicatessens. Either way, they are expensive; but their flavor is so special, it is well worth the occasional splurge. In addition, a little bit goes a long way, especially when wild varieties are mixed with more interesting cultivated mushrooms, such as oyster or shiitake.

Cultivated Mushrooms

Button mushroom The youngest stage of the common cultivated white mushroom and almost all cap, these are picked when they have just come through the earth. They are best suited to salads, soups, marinades, and sauces, where their mild flavor serves as a good vehicle for other flavorings such as garlic, herbs, and spices.

Open cup This is the next stage of the cultivated button mushroom. In the mature mushroom the gills are visible, as is the stem. They are good for baking and general flavoring, and make excellent additions to stuffings. If the stems are not needed for a recipe, reserve them for stock, as they have a lot of flavor.

Flat This is the final stage of the cultivated white variety, in which the cap has opened out completely. These "old" mushrooms have a very pronounced flavor and are excellent in soups, stews, pâtés, or broiled and served with bacon and eggs.

Brown cap Also known as chestnut, Italian field, or cremini, this variety of cultivated mushroom looks like the button or open cup, but has a brown cap. It has a fuller flavor and is a good all-purpose variety.

Cultivated Wild Mushrooms

Oyster Originally a wild variety, this mushroom is now successfully cultivated, and is quite widely available. It has a fan shape, with a pale color and good flavor. Use in a stir-fry or mixed with other types, or sauté with a little butter and garlic. Pink and yellow varieties are also available, but there is no difference in flavor.

Enoki These delicate, threadlike, cultivated mushrooms are native to Japan. With their long stems and tiny caps, they resemble bean sprouts. They are best eaten raw — as a garnish or in salads — or cooked briefly as a last-minute addition to soups.

Shiitake A favorite Oriental mushroom which, like the oyster, is now being cultivated. The cap is brown, thin-textured, and velvety, with a slim white stalk that is tough and best discarded. The shiitake has a pronounced flavor and meaty texture, and can be stir-fried or used in casseroles and sauces, or combined with other less flavorful varieties. It can also be purchased dried, most commonly in Asian or specialty supermarkets.

Wild Mushrooms

Wood-ear Also known as cloud-ear, these mushrooms have shiny brown jellylike tops with dry tan undersides. They are available fresh, mainly in specialty markets, or dried. Essentially stemless, they are used in Chinese cuisine, more for texture than for flavor.

Porcini Also known as cèpe, this is the supreme wild mushroom, with a superlative taste and texture. It has a round, brown cap with a spongy underside, growing from a chubby stem. It can grow to enormous proportions (however, the big ones don't necessarily have the best flavor). As with most wild mushrooms, these are not ideal for eating raw.

Chanterelle Perhaps the second most popular of the wild mushrooms, the chanterelle is a very pretty variety, with color ranging from yellow to deep orange. Its concave cap, with fluted edge, sits atop a thin, tapering stem. Chanterelles have an earthy flavor and are delicious with chicken, fish, and in warm salads, or, as with all wild varieties, sautéed in butter or oil and served alone.

STORAGE & PREPARATION

Fresh mushrooms do not keep well. They do best stored in the refrigerator or somewhere cool, preferably in a paper bag, but not in plastic, where they will become slimy. Keep for a maximum of three days. Mushrooms past their prime can be used in broth or soup.

When preparing and cleaning mushrooms, take care not to bruise them. Avoid washing mushrooms, as it spoils the flavor and texture. Usually, cultivated varieties do not need washing, so a quick rinse in a strainer or with a soft mushroom brush will do. Wipe dry with some paper towels to remove any humus clinging to the cap. Wild mushrooms need a little more attention: cut off the gritty base of the stem; remove any debris with a soft brush; cut out any damaged areas; then rinse, but only briefly (otherwise they become soggy). Dry with paper towels as above.

Many varieties of wild mushrooms are available dried, and are a marvelous addition to soups, stews, or breads. They will keep almost indefinitely in a cool dark cupboard. Simply reconstitute in warm water, drain, rinse, and use as needed. Keep the soaking water, as it retains lots of flavor from the mushrooms, and use it, strained of any grit, in cooking.

DRYING MUSHROOMS AT HOME

If you have a glut of mushrooms, a good way of preserving them is to dry them. First, clean the mushrooms as described above. Large specimens, such as porcini, should be sliced.

The simplest method is to use a large needle to thread the mushrooms onto a string, tying a knot between each one. Hang them over a radiator, heater, or some other warm place — a warm, dry cupboard is ideal — until shriveled and dry.

Another method is to dry mushrooms in the oven. Set a wire rack on top of a baking sheet lined with newspaper. Spread the mushrooms out in an even layer, and put in a warm (140°F–150°F) oven, leaving the door ajar to let any moisture escape. Bake until the mushrooms are completely dry and leathery (they will shrink too). Cool completely, then store the dried mushrooms in airtight containers in a cool, dark place.

STARTERS

Wild Mushroom Soup with Parmesan Croûtons

1 ounce dried porcini mushrooms

5 cups warm water

3 tablespoons olive oil

4 shallots, chopped

2 garlic cloves, crushed or minced

1½ pounds brown cap mushrooms, coarsely chopped

2 cups vegetable broth

½ teaspoon each salt and freshly ground black pepper

1 tablespoon whole grain mustard

3 tablespoons minced fresh parsley

Croûtons

3 slices heavy Italian or French country-style bread, crusts removed

Oil for frying

¼ cup freshly grated Parmesan cheese

Soak the dried mushrooms in the water for 30 minutes. Drain, reserve the liquid, then rinse thoroughly under cold running water. Chop coarsely and set aside. Strain the liquid through a paper coffee filter or a piece of cheesecloth to remove any grit.

Heat the oil in a large saucepan. Add the shallots and garlic, and sauté gently until softened. Add the soaked mushrooms and continue cooking for 5 minutes. Stir in the brown cap mushrooms and cook, stirring, for about 10 minutes. Add the broth and seasoning, bring to a boil, then reduce heat, cover, and simmer for 45 minutes, or until the dried mushrooms are tender.

Meanwhile, to make the croûtons, cut the slices of bread into small cubes. Heat about 1 inch of oil in a deep skillet. (The oil will have reached the correct temperature when a piece of added bread sizzles immediately.) Add the bread cubes and fry until golden. Remove with a slotted spoon and drain on paper towels. While the croûtons are still warm, toss them with the Parmesan cheese.

Transfer the soup to a blender or food processor — you may have to do this in batches — and purée until smooth. Return to the pan, stir in the mustard, half the reserved mushroom liquid, and taste for seasoning. Serve with the Parmesan croûtons and garnish with the minced parsley. *Serves 4.*

Grilled Polenta with Wild Mushrooms & Taleggio

6 cups water

1¼ teaspoons salt

1½ cups quick-cooking polenta

6 ounces Taleggio cheese

2 tablespoons freshly grated Parmesan cheese

2 tablespoons olive oil

1 garlic clove, halved

1 pound wild mushrooms, such as porcini, oyster,
chanterelle, wiped and sliced

¼ teaspoon freshly ground black pepper

1 tablespoon minced fresh parsley

8 large basil leaves, thinly sliced

*B*ring the water and 1 teaspoon of the salt to a boil in a large heavy-bottomed saucepan. When the water boils, add the polenta in a thin stream, stirring constantly as you do so. Stir and cook for 4 minutes, then remove from the heat. Cut 4 ounces of the Taleggio cheese into

14

cubes, and stir into the hot polenta with the Parmesan cheese. Lightly oil a 4×8-inch loaf pan and pour the polenta into it, leveling the surface. Let cool for 15 minutes.

Heat the olive oil in a sauté pan, and add the garlic. Cook until golden, then discard the garlic — it will have flavored the oil. Add the mushrooms and sauté for 5 minutes, or until they just begin to release their juices. Stir in the remaining salt, the pepper, and the minced parsley.

Preheat the broiler. Turn the cooled polenta out of the loaf pan, trim the edges, and cut into 8 slices. Place under the broiler, and broil for 4–5 minutes, until golden and crisp on the outside.

Cut the remaining Taleggio into thin slices. Sauté the mushrooms for 1 minute over high heat to warm. Put 2 slices of polenta on each plate, spoon over the hot mushrooms, and top with the slices of Taleggio. Serve with the basil leaves sprinkled on top. *Serves 4.*

NOTE Making polenta the traditional way is a laborious exercise. Quick-cooking polenta is available in Italian delicatessens and some large supermarkets. Cooking instructions may vary by brand, so follow the manufacturers' suggestions.

Mushroom & Chicken Terrine

1 pound button mushrooms, sliced

1/4 pound boneless chicken, diced

3/4 cup fresh white bread crumbs

1/2 egg white

1/2 cup heavy cream

1 tablespoon butter

1/2 cup minced shallots

1 clove garlic, crushed or minced

2/3 cup fresh chicken broth

1/2 teaspoon ground cumin

3 teaspoons minced fresh chives

1 teaspoon salt and 1/2 teaspoon
freshly ground black pepper

4 bay leaves

12 ounces bacon

Fresh baby spinach leaves

*H*eat a heavy-bottomed skillet, add the mushrooms, and dry fry, stirring continuously to prevent sticking, until thoroughly cooked. Drain in a strainer and let cool.

Put the chicken, bread crumbs, egg white, and cream into a food processor. Whirl to a smooth purée. Cover and keep chilled.

Melt the butter in a small pan over low heat. Add the shallots and garlic, and cook until soft. Add the chicken broth and cumin. Raise the heat to high and boil until liquid is reduced by half. Strain the mixture, discard the shallots, and reserve the liquid.

In a mixing bowl, combine the cooked mushrooms, chicken mixture, and reduced broth. Add 2 teaspoons of the minced chives, and the seasoning. Mix until thoroughly combined.

Preheat the oven to 350°F. Arrange the bay leaves on the bottom of a buttered 2½-cup terrine mold or 4×8-inch loaf pan.

Line with the bacon, allowing the ends to hang over the sides. Spoon the mixture into the pan, making sure it fills the corners and sides, without leaving any gaps. Cover with any remaining bacon and fold the ends in. Cover with buttered wax paper and a tight-fitting lid, or double layer of foil. Put the terrine in a roasting pan filled with about 1 inch of hot water. Bake in the oven for 45 minutes, or just until firm to the touch. Remove from the roasting pan, let cool, remove the bay leaves, then chill.

Serve the terrine in slices, on a bed of fresh baby spinach leaves, garnished with the remaining chives. *Serves 4.*

NOTE Other herbs — chervil or tarragon are good alternatives — can be used in place of chives.

Little Fila Mushrooms

4 tablespoons butter

2 small shallots, minced

½ red bell pepper, finely diced

3 slices bacon, diced

1 cup chopped brown cap
  mushrooms

½ teaspoon each salt and freshly
  ground black pepper

½ cup diced mozzarella cheese

3–4 sheets fila pastry

Frisée lettuce, shredded

½ red bell pepper, cut into strips

*T*o make the filling, melt 1 tablespoon of the butter in a
skillet, add the shallots and diced red bell pepper, and
cook until soft. Add the bacon, and cook for 5 minutes more.
Add the mushrooms and cook until the liquid has evaporated.
Season, then stir in the mozzarella. Let cool.

Preheat the oven to 375°F. Melt the remaining butter. Brush
one sheet of pastry with butter, then cut crosswise into four
rectangular strips.
Place a large spoonful
of the mushroom
mixture at one narrow
end of each strip of
pastry. Fold in the
edges of the long
sides, then roll the
pastry up around the

filling. The result should be a neatly wrapped cylinder, sealed at both ends to enclose the mushroom mixture.

Place the cylinders, sitting upright, on a greased or nonstick baking sheet, pressing them down gently. Repeat with one more sheet of fila pastry. Bake for 15–20 minutes, until golden.

Using a 3-inch round pastry cutter, or the rim of a water glass, cut out 24 circles from the remaining pastry. Use the circles to line 8 shallow muffin pans, layering three circles in each, and brushing melted butter between each layer. Bake for 10 minutes until golden.

To assemble the "mushrooms," place two "stems" (the filled pastries) on each plate and top each one with a "cap" (the pastry circles). Surround the pastries with frisée lettuce, garnished with the red pepper strips. Serve warm. *Serves 4.*

NOTE To make these whimsical pies even more delicious, put a teaspoonful of truffle paste (*crema di tartufi* — available in good Italian delicatessens), or mascarpone cheese, beaten with minced fresh herbs, on top of the stems, before putting on the caps.

19

Mushroom Ragoût with Toasted Brioche

4 tablespoons butter

2 shallots, minced

1 pound mixed mushrooms, such as
   shiitake, oyster, and chanterelle,
   wiped, trimmed and sliced

4 tomatoes

2 tablespoons minced fresh chives

½ teaspoon each salt and freshly
   ground black pepper

3 tablespoons crème fraîche

8 slices brioche, toasted

*M*elt the butter in a large skillet over medium heat, add the shallots, and cook until softened. Add the mushrooms and cook, covered, for 5 minutes, until softened.

Plunge the tomatoes into boiling water for 30 seconds, then into cold water. Peel, cut into quarters, remove the seeds, and chop coarsely.

Add the tomatoes and half the chives to the mushroom mixture. Simmer until thickened. Add the seasoning and stir in the crème fraîche.

Serve the ragoût spooned over the slices of toasted brioche, allowing 2 slices per person, and garnish with the remaining chives.

Serves 4.

Mixed Mushroom Tempura

Batter

1 cup all-purpose flour

1 teaspoon baking powder

1 egg yolk

1½ cups ice water

Dipping Sauce

¼ cup mirin or medium sherry

¼ cup light soy sauce

1 cup chicken broth

½ teaspoon chopped fresh ginger

Vegetable oil for deep frying

About 14 ounces enoki mushrooms,
   root ends trimmed

8 shiitake mushrooms

8 large oyster mushrooms

8 large brown cap mushrooms, sliced

Sift the flour and baking powder into a bowl. Mix the egg yolk with the water, then gradually add to the flour mixture, beating until smooth. Set aside in a cool place until ready to use.

To make the sauce, gently heat the ingredients together in a small pan; keep warm.

Half fill a wok or deep pan with the oil, and heat to 375°F. Dip the mushrooms, a few at a time, into the batter and fry until golden, 1–2 minutes. Drain on paper towels and serve hot with the sauce. *Serves 4.*

21

Chinese Mushroom & Cellophane Noodle Salad

2 garlic cloves, crushed or minced

1 tablespoon rice vinegar

1 tablespoon light soy sauce

3 tablespoons sugar

2 small red Thai chiles, seeded and finely sliced

1 tablespoon sesame oil

¼ teaspoon freshly ground pepper

½ pound shiitake mushrooms, thinly sliced

5 dried wood-ear mushrooms, softened in hot water and drained

2 ounces cellophane noodles or bean threads, cut into 4-inch lengths

1 large carrot, cut into matchsticks

1 large zucchini, cut into matchsticks

1 tablespoon toasted sesame seeds

2 tablespoons chopped fresh cilantro

Mix the garlic, vinegar, soy sauce, sugar, chiles, sesame oil, and pepper in a bowl. Add the shiitake and wood-ear mushrooms, and mix well.

Cook the noodles in boiling water for 1 minute. Drain thoroughly and refresh under cold running water. Drain again.

Add the carrot and zucchini to the mushrooms, then mix in the noodles. Stir well to coat the ingredients with the dressing. Sprinkle with the sesame seeds. Serve at room temperature, garnished with the cilantro. *Serves 4.*

NOTE Cellophane noodles are also known as translucent, shining, or *harusame* noodles and are available at Asian supermarkets — as are the wood-ear mushrooms also known as cloud- or tree-ears, or black Fungus. If fresh shiitake mushrooms are unavailable, dried ones can be used. Soak in hot water, as with the cloud-ears.

Mushroom Pâté

8 ounces cream cheese
1 tablespoon Madeira
¼ cup butter
¾ cup chopped shallots
1 pound brown cap or button mushrooms, chopped
1 tablespoon anchovy paste
¼ teaspoon cayenne
1 cup chopped parsley

Place the cream cheese and the Madeira in an electric blender or food processor and whirl until creamed.

Melt the butter in a large skillet over medium heat. Add the shallots and cook gently until softened. Add the mushrooms, anchovy paste, and cayenne. Cook, stirring occasionally, until the mushrooms are limp. Using a slotted spoon, add the hot mushroom mixture and the parsley to the cream cheese and process, using on-off pulses, just until all the ingredients are blended.

Spoon into a terrine or deep serving dish and refrigerate until firm. Store in the refrigerator for up to 1 week. *Serves 4.*

NOTE This pâté is delicious spread on toast. It's also very good in a turkey or chicken sandwich.

Hot & Sour Mushroom Soup

4¼ cups chicken broth
1 stalk lemongrass, chopped
1 tablespoon grated lime zest
¼ teaspoon salt
¼ cup fresh lime juice
¼ teaspoon chili paste (sambal)
¼ teaspoon sugar
About 7 ounces enoki mushrooms,
  root ends trimmed

¼ pound bean sprouts
1 bunch scallions, thinly sliced
½ pound large shrimp, peeled and
  deveined
2 small red Thai chiles, seeded and
  thinly sliced
¼ cup fresh cilantro leaves

*P*ut the broth, lemongrass, and lime zest in a large pan. Bring to a boil; reduce heat and simmer for 15 minutes. Strain the broth and return to the pan. Season with the salt, then add the lime juice, chili paste, and sugar. Add the mushrooms, bean sprouts, and scallions, and simmer for 1 minute. Add the shrimp and simmer for 5 minutes more, or until the shrimp are pink. Serve sprinkled with the chiles and cilantro. *Serves 4.*

Mushroom Omelet

4 tablespoons olive oil

¾ pound brown cap mushrooms, sliced

3 cloves garlic, crushed or minced

¼ cup finely chopped fresh parsley

4 slices wafer-thin Parma ham, finely diced

6 eggs

½ teaspoon each salt and freshly ground black pepper

12 cherry tomatoes, halved

*H*eat 2 tablespoons of the oil in a deep skillet or omelet pan. Add the mushrooms, garlic, parsley, and ham, and cook over high heat for 2–3 minutes, until just browned.

Beat the eggs in a bowl and add the mushroom mixture. Season with the salt and pepper. Wipe the pan, then add the remaining oil. When it is hot, pour in the egg and mushroom mixture. Lower the heat and cook until the underside of the omelet is brown and just set. Place a plate face down over the

omelet and turn out, then return the omelet to the pan, with the browned side up. Continue cooking until the omelet is browned again on the bottom. Serve warm, cut into wedges, garnished with the tomatoes. *Serves 4.*

MAIN DISHES

Chicken with Oyster Mushrooms & Lemon

1 chicken (about 4 pounds), cut into
  eighths
1/4–1/3 cup all-purpose flour
1/3 cup olive oil
2 onions, thinly sliced
2 cloves garlic, crushed or minced
1 1/4 cups dry white wine
2/3 cup chicken broth
1/2 teaspoon each salt and freshly
  ground black pepper

1/2 pound oyster mushrooms, halved
  if large
1 bay leaf
3 tablespoons minced fresh parsley
1 can (about 1 pound) artichoke
  hearts, drained and rinsed
1 lemon, thinly sliced
1 tablespoons chopped fresh basil

*D*ust the chicken pieces with the flour. In a large skillet, heat the oil over medium heat. Add the chicken and cook until browned all over. Remove the chicken and set aside.

Add the onions and cook over low heat until softened. Add the garlic and cook for 3–4 minutes more. Stir in the wine and broth, then the seasoning. Add the chicken, mushrooms, bay leaf, and parsley. Cover and simmer for 15 minutes. Stir in the artichokes, and lay the lemon on top. Cover, and cook for about 15 minutes, until the chicken is cooked through. Add the basil. *Serves 4.*

Roast Fillet of Beef with Wild Mushrooms

Madeira Sauce

1³/₄ cups red wine

¹/₄ cup Madeira

¹/₄ cup balsamic vinegar

10 small or 5 large shallots, sliced

1 bay leaf

1 thyme sprig

1¹/₂ cups beef or veal broth

2 tablespoons butter

1 tablespoon oil

1¹/₂ pound piece fillet of beef,
  trimmed

1 shallot, minced

2 tablespoons butter

2 cups mixed wild mushrooms,
  such as porcini or chanterelles,
  cleaned, trimmed, and sliced

¹/₂ cup cooked or canned chestnuts,
  peeled and halved

2 sun-dried tomatoes packed in oil,
  cut into thin slivers

3 tablespoons minced fresh parsley

Large pinch each salt and freshly
  ground black pepper

Few chervil sprigs

*T*o make the Madeira sauce, put the red wine, Madeira, balsamic vinegar, sliced shallots, bay leaf, and thyme into a bowl. Let stand for 2–3 hours. Transfer the liquid to a saucepan, bring to a boil, and reduce to one-third of the original volume. Remove the bay leaf and thyme, add the broth, bring to a boil again, and reduce by half. Set aside.

Preheat the oven to 400°F. Heat the oil in a heavy-bottomed skillet, add the fillet, and brown over high heat. Transfer the fillet to a roasting pan and roast for 25 minutes for medium-rare. Remove from the oven and let rest, covered, for 10 minutes.

Meanwhile, in a skillet, combine the minced shallot and butter and cook over low heat until soft. Add the mushrooms and sauté until all liquid has evaporated. Stir in the chestnuts, sun-dried tomatoes, parsley, and seasoning. Set aside. Reheat the sauce over very low heat, adding the remaining butter and stirring until incorporated; do not let the sauce boil. Sauté the mushroom mixture briefly over high heat to warm through.

Cut the beef into four thick slices and put on heated plates. Spoon a little of the sauce around the meat and surround with the mushroom mixture. Garnish with the chervil and serve immediately. *Serves 4.*

Duck, Mushroom & Black Bean Stir-fry

1½ pounds boneless duck breast halves

½ teaspoon salt

½ teaspoon sugar

1 tablespoon soy sauce

2 teaspoons rice wine or dry sherry

1 teaspoon cornstarch

1 small egg white

1 tablespoon vegetable oil

3 cloves garlic, sliced

1-inch piece fresh ginger, peeled and cut into slivers

3 tablespoons canned black beans, rinsed and drained

1 each green and red bell peppers, thinly sliced

1¼ pound snow peas, trimmed

½ pound oyster mushrooms, thickly sliced if large

3 scallions, sliced diagonally

1 cup long-grain rice, cooked

Few cilantro sprigs

Remove the skin from the duck breasts and slice it into thin strips. Cut the duck meat crosswise into thin slices.

In a bowl, combine the salt, sugar, soy sauce, rice wine, and cornstarch. Beat in the egg white. Add the duck meat, turn to coat, and let marinate for 15 minutes.

Heat a wok over high heat and add the strips of duck skin. Stir-fry until crispy and golden. Remove with a slotted spoon and drain on paper towels. Pour out the fat and wipe the wok clean with paper towels.

Heat the oil in the wok. Add the garlic and ginger, and stir-fry for 30 seconds. Add the duck slices, marinade, and black beans and stir-fry for 1 minute. Remove and set aside. Add the bell peppers and snow peas and stir-fry for 2–3 minutes. Add the mushrooms and stir-fry for 1 minute. Return the duck and black beans to the wok and stir-fry for 2 minutes more, adding a little water if needed. Serve with rice, garnished with the crispy duck skin, the scallions, and the cilantro. *Serves 4.*

Eggplant, Mushroom & Tofu Brochettes

1 medium-size eggplant

Coarse or kosher salt

1 tablespoon sesame oil

3 tablespoons light soy sauce

1 tablespoon honey

1 teaspoon chili oil

16 button mushrooms, wiped

½ pound tofu, cut into 16 cubes

8 large cloves garlic, unpeeled

1 large red bell pepper, cored,
    seeded, and cut into 8 or 16 chunks

Zest of 1 orange, cut into
    julienne strips

Sweet and Sour Sauce

¼ cup sugar

¼ cup rice vinegar

3 tablespoons dark soy sauce

3 tablespoons cornstarch

3 tablespoons tomato paste

⅔ cup fresh orange juice

¾ cup water

Cut the eggplant into chunks about the same size as the mushrooms (try to cut an even number — enough to make 8 brochettes). Put the chunks into a strainer and sprinkle with salt. Let stand for 30 minutes to extract the bitter juices.

In a bowl, mix the sesame oil, soy sauce, honey, and chili oil, then add to the mushrooms and tofu. Toss to coat ingredients. Marinate for 30 minutes.

Put the unpeeled garlic cloves in boiling water and cook for 10–15 minutes. Drain and let cool.

Rinse the eggplant and pat dry.

32

Thread the eggplant, mushrooms, tofu, garlic cloves, and pepper onto eight wooden or metal skewers. Preheat the broiler and cook the brochettes, turning them often for about 20 minutes, or until browned and the vegetables are tender.

Meanwhile, to make the sauce, put all the ingredients into a saucepan. Cook, stirring, over medium heat until thick, translucent, and glossy.

Serve the brochettes hot, with sauce spooned over them and garnished with the julienned orange zest. *Serves 4.*

NOTE These brochettes can be cooked on the barbecue. Serve them with rice or baked potatoes.

Chèvre, Mushroom & Walnut Tart

1¼ cups all-purpose flour
¼ cup butter

Filling

2 tablespoons butter
1 clove garlic, crushed or minced
1 pound sliced mixed mushrooms
3 sun-dried tomatoes packed in oil, cut into thin slivers
1 log chèvre cheese (about 5½ ounces), sliced into 6–8 rounds
Large pinch each salt and freshly ground black pepper
¼ cup walnuts, chopped
6 large fresh basil leaves, thinly sliced
2 eggs
1 cup milk

*P*reheat the oven to 375°F. Put the flour in a bowl, add the butter, and rub in, using your fingertips, until the mixture resembles fine bread crumbs. Add 2–3 tablespoons cold water, and knead gently to form a dough. Wrap and refrigerate for 15 minutes.

Roll out the pastry and fit it into an 8-inch pie plate. Trim the edges,

34

prick the bottom with a fork, and refrigerate for 10 minutes. Line the pastry shell with foil or wax paper, fill with dry beans, and bake for 15 minutes. Remove the lining and beans, and return the pastry to the oven for 5 minutes more.

For the filling, melt the butter in a medium skillet, add the garlic and mushrooms, and cook for 5 minutes, stirring, until the moisture from the mushrooms has evaporated. Spoon into the pastry shell. Arrange first the sun-dried tomatoes, then the chèvre on top of the mushrooms.

Season the tart, then sprinkle with the walnuts and basil. Beat the eggs with the milk, then pour over the mushroom mixture. Bake for 20–25 minutes, just until set and lightly golden. Serve warm. *Serves 4.*

NOTE A crisp green salad is the perfect accompaniment.

Spicy Bean, Mushroom & Chorizo Stew

3 tablespoons olive oil

1 onion, chopped

2 cloves garlic, crushed or minced

1 small red bell pepper, chopped

1¾ cups peeled, seeded, and diced tomatoes

1 tablespoon tomato paste

3 tablespoons canned chopped green chiles

1 tablespoon molasses

1 tablespoon brown sugar

1 bay leaf

½ teaspoon each salt and freshly ground black pepper

2½ cups cooked black-eyed peas

½ pound chorizo, Italian, or other spicy sausage, thickly sliced

½ pound shiitake mushrooms, sliced

1½ cups fresh bread crumbs

¼ cup freshly grated Parmesan cheese

4 baked potatoes

Sour cream

*H*eat the oil in a heavy-bottomed skillet. Add the onion, garlic, and bell pepper, and cook until soft and golden.

Add the tomatoes, tomato paste, chiles, molasses, brown sugar, bay leaf, and seasoning. Cover and simmer for 15 minutes.

Add the black-eyed peas, sausage, and mushrooms. Continue to cook for 10–15 minutes more.

Preheat the broiler. Transfer the mixture to an ovenproof dish, and sprinkle with the bread crumbs and Parmesan cheese. Broil until the bread crumbs have turned golden brown and crisp. Serve with baked potatoes and sour cream. *Serves 4.*

NOTE Chorizo is a spicy Spanish sausage, available in good delicatessens. If unavailable, substitute any good, firm, spicy sausage, such as merguez, pepperoni, or garlic sausage.

Mushroom, Red Onion & Sun-dried Tomato Pizzas

Pizza Dough

1 package active dry yeast

⅔ cup warm water

2 teaspoons sugar

½ teaspoon salt

3 tablespoons olive oil

1¾ cups all-purpose flour

2 tablespoons olive oil

2 tablespoons butter

2 medium red onions, thinly sliced

⅓ cup Black Olive Paste (page 56)

½ pound shiitake mushrooms, sliced

8–10 sun-dried tomatoes packed in oil, cut into slivers

½ pound mozzarella cheese, coarsely chopped

3 tablespoons pine nuts

2 cloves garlic, thinly sliced

1 teaspoon crushed red pepper flakes

Freshly ground black pepper

4 tablespoons oil from the sun-dried tomatoes

1 tablespoon chopped fresh parsley

*T*o make the dough, mix the yeast and water in a large bowl; let stand for 5 minutes. Stir in the sugar, salt, and oil. Add 1⅓ cups of the flour and mix for about 5 minutes, until elastic. Stir in about ½ cup more flour to make a soft dough. Knead on a lightly floured surface for about 10 minutes until smooth. Put in a greased bowl, cover, and let rise in a warm place for about 45 minutes, until doubled in size.

Meanwhile, heat the oil and butter in a skillet. Add the onions and cook gently over low heat, covered, for about 10 minutes, until soft. Let cool.

Preheat the oven to 450°F. Divide the dough into four equal pieces and roll each into a 7-inch round.

Heat a heavy-bottomed nonstick skillet large enough to hold one pizza, then cook each crust about 1½–2 minutes on each side, until it begins to brown and crisp. Put the pizza crusts on baking sheets.

Spread the Black Olive Paste evenly over each crust, then top with the cooked onions, the mushrooms, sun-dried tomatoes, and mozzarella cheese. Sprinkle with the pine nuts, garlic, and red pepper flakes. Season with black pepper. Drizzle each pizza with a tablespoon of tomato oil. Bake on the middle rack of the oven for 8–10 minutes, or until the cheese has just melted. Sprinkle with parsley before serving. *Serves 4.*

Spiced Mushrooms, Smoked Mussels & Spinach with Couscous

4 tablespoons butter

1 medium onion, chopped

2 cloves garlic, crushed or minced

1 teaspoon tomato paste

½ teaspoon ground coriander

½ teaspoon ground cumin

¼ teaspoon cayenne

¼ teaspoon turmeric

¾ pound button mushrooms, whole

⅔ cup cooked garbanzo beans

½ pound baby spinach leaves, washed

½ teaspoon each salt and freshly ground black pepper

1 can (about 3½ ounces) smoked mussels, drained

2 tablespoons chopped fresh cilantro

Couscous

1¾ cups water

½ teaspoon salt

1 tablespoon oil

1⅓ cup couscous

*M*elt 2 tablespoons of the butter in a large skillet. Add the onion and cook until golden. Add the garlic and cook for 1 minute more. Stir in the tomato paste, coriander, cumin, cayenne, and turmeric; cook and stir for 2 minutes. Add the mushrooms and sauté until they begin to give off moisture. Add the garbanzo beans and stir well. If the mixture seems a little dry, add some water. Cover and cook for 10 minutes.

To make the couscous, bring the water to a boil in a large saucepan. Add the salt and oil. Pour in the couscous, turn off the heat, stir, cover, and let stand for 5 minutes.

Add the spinach to the mushroom mixture, stir well, and cook just until the leaves have wilted. Add the seasoning and gently stir in the mussels.

Add the remaining 2 tablespoons butter to the couscous and cook over medium heat, stirring, for about 5 minutes. Separate the grains with a fork, then transfer the couscous to a serving platter. Spoon the mushroom and spinach mixture on top and sprinkle with cilantro. *Serves 4.*

NOTE If smoked mussels are unavailable, use 12–16 fresh mussels in the shell. Add them after the spinach, cover the pan, and cook for about 5 minutes. Discard any that remain closed.

Tuna Steaks with Porcini, Baby Onions & Potatoes

4 tablespoons unsalted butter

6 tablespoons olive oil

12 baby onions, peeled

20 small potatoes

1 teaspoon each salt and freshly ground black pepper

4 large fresh porcini mushrooms, wiped and trimmed

¼ cup minced fresh parsley

4 fresh tuna steaks (about 6 ounces each)

1 lemon, cut into 8 wedges

Few parsley sprigs

*H*eat 2 tablespoons of the butter and 2 tablespoons of the oil in a large nonstick skillet. When hot, stir in the onions and potatoes and cook gently until just beginning to turn golden. Lower the heat, season with half the salt and pepper, and continue cooking for about 10 minutes.

Heat the remaining 2 tablespoons butter in another skillet. Add the porcini and cook for 6 minutes. Remove from the skillet, cut each mushroom in six wedges, and add to the potato mixture. Stir in the parsley, then transfer the mixture to a warm serving dish. Cover with foil to keep warm.

Heat the remaining 4 tablespoons oil in a large nonstick skillet. Season the tuna steaks with the remaining salt and pepper, then add to the skillet and cook until dark golden, turning once to brown both sides (about 5 minutes per side). Arrange the steaks on top of the vegetables. Serve immediately, garnished with the lemon wedges and parsley. *Serves 4.*

NOTE The tuna steaks can also be cooked on the barbecue or under the broiler. Cooking time will still be about 5 minutes per side. Salmon steaks can be used in place of the tuna.

Mushroom Gnocchi

2 ounces dried porcini mushrooms	1 tablespoon tomato paste
5 cups warm water	1 pound russet potatoes, peeled
1/4 cup plus 2 tablespoons butter	3/4 cup all-purpose flour
1/4 cup olive oil	Pinch of ground nutmeg
1 clove garlic, crushed or minced	2 tablespoons freshly grated
1 tablespoon chopped fresh parsley	Parmesan cheese
1/2 cup red wine	Few parsley sprigs
1/2 teaspoon each salt and freshly ground black pepper	

Soak the mushrooms in the water for 30 minutes. Drain, reserving the liquid. Rinse the mushrooms thoroughly. Strain the liquid through a paper coffee filter or a piece of cheesecloth to remove any grit.

Melt 2 tablespoons of the butter with the olive oil in a large skillet. Add the garlic and parsley, and cook over low heat for 5 minutes, stirring. Add the mushrooms and stir for 10 minutes more, then add the wine and season with half the salt and pepper. Cook for about 10 minutes, until the wine has almost completely evaporated. Add the tomato paste and cook for 15 minutes more, stirring occasionally. The mixture should be thick. Let cool slightly, then transfer to a food processor or blender and purée until smooth.

Cook the potatoes in boiling, salted water until tender, but not mushy. Drain thoroughly, then mash until smooth.

To make the gnocchi, sift the flour into a large bowl and make a well in the center. Add the potatoes and mushroom mixture. Add the remaining seasoning and the nutmeg. Using your hands, gradually knead the flour into the mushroom and potato, until a dough is formed. On a floured board, shape the dough into long rolls about 1 inch in diameter, then cut into ½-inch pieces. Melt the remaining ¼ cup butter.

Put the reserved mushroom liquid in a large pan, and add enough water to make 3 quarts. Add salt and bring to a boil. Gently drop the gnocchi into the water and poach for about 1 minute after they have risen to the surface. Using a slotted spoon, transfer the gnocchi to a serving dish and pour over the melted butter. Sprinkle with the Parmesan and garnish with the parsley. Serve immediately. *Serves 4.*

Mushroom-flavored Tagliatelle

1 ounce dried porcini mushrooms

5 cups warm water

2 cloves garlic, crushed or minced

1 tablespoon minced fresh parsley

6 tablespoons olive oil

½ teaspoon each salt and freshly ground black pepper

1¼ pound pasta flour or bread flour

2 large eggs

5 tablespoons melted butter

4 tablespoons freshly grated Parmesan cheese

2 tablespoons chopped fresh parsley

Soak the porcini mushrooms in the warm water for 30 minutes. Drain, reserving the liquid. Rinse the mushrooms thoroughly. Strain the liquid through a paper coffee filter or a piece of cheesecloth to remove any grit.

Chop the mushrooms very finely and mix with the garlic, parsley, and oil. Transfer the mixture to a small pan and add 1 cup of the mushroom liquid. Season with half the salt and the pepper, and simmer for 30 minutes, stirring occasionally. Let cool completely.

To make the tagliatelle, sift the flour onto a wooden board or clean work surface. Make a well in the center and add the mushroom purée and eggs. Using the fingers of one hand, mix the purée and eggs, then gradually draw in the flour until the mixture forms a stiff dough. Knead until smooth and elastic (about 15 minutes). Wrap and let stand in a cool place for 1 hour.

Divide the dough into quarters. Working one at a time, roll out the dough pieces until paper thin. Sprinkle with a little flour and roll the pasta up. With a sharp knife, cut crosswise into ribbons about ½-inch wide. Unroll the ribbons and lay them out on a wire rack or dry dishtowel. Let sit for 30 minutes before cooking.

Put the remaining mushroom liquid into a large pan, then add enough cold water to make 3 quarts. Add the remaining salt and bring to a boil. Add the tagliatelle and cook for about 3 minutes, or until "al dente." Drain, then toss with the melted butter, Parmesan cheese, and parsley. *Serves 4.*

NOTE This pasta has such a pronounced flavor it should be served simply, as suggested.

SIDE DISHES

Mixed Grain & Mushroom Pilaf

2 tablespoons butter

1 tablespoon olive oil

1 cup finely sliced mixed wild mushrooms,

such as oyster, chanterelle, and shiitake

3 shallots, minced

2 cloves garlic, thinly sliced

⅓ cup dry white wine

4 tablespoons whole grain barley

3 cups chicken broth

⅓ cup medium buckwheat groats (kasha)

½ teaspoon each salt and freshly ground black pepper

¼ pound asparagus, trimmed, sliced into 2-inch lengths, and blanched

¼ cup minced fresh cilantro

*M*elt half the butter with the olive oil in a skillet. Add the mushrooms and cook, stirring, over high heat until just beginning to brown. Remove from the pan and set aside.

Reduce heat and melt the remaining butter in the same skillet. Add the shallots and cook for about 1 minute. Add the garlic and cook for 2 minutes more. Add the wine and increase the heat. As the wine boils, scrape the bottom of the pan to loosen any bits. Boil until the liquid is reduced to 3 tablespoons.

Reduce the heat and stir in the barley. Add the broth and simmer for about 1½ hours, or until the barley is cooked.

Stir in the mushrooms, buckwheat, and seasoning, and continue cooking for 15–20 minutes, until the buckwheat is tender. Stir in the asparagus and cook for 1 minute. Stir in the chopped cilantro. Serve hot with roast meats or game. *Serves 4.*

Risotto with Porcini

1 ounce dried porcini mushrooms

2 cups warm water

3 tablespoons butter

3 tablespoons olive oil

2 shallots, finely chopped

2 cups arborio rice

5 cups hot chicken or veal broth

½ teaspoon each salt and freshly ground black pepper

½ cup freshly grated Parmesan cheese

2 tablespoons minced fresh parsley

Soak the mushrooms in the water for 20 minutes. Drain and chop, reserving the liquid. Rinse the mushrooms thoroughly. Strain the liquid through a paper coffee filter or a piece of cheesecloth to remove any grit.

Heat 1 tablespoon of the butter and the olive oil in a large heavy-bottomed saucepan. Add the shallots and cook over medium heat until softened, then add the rice and stir to coat.

Add ½ cup of the hot broth (keep it gently simmering in another saucepan) to the rice, and cook, stirring, until the liquid has been absorbed. Continue adding the broth in this manner, until the rice has cooked for about 15 minutes. Add the mushrooms and half the reserved liquid. Continue cooking and stirring, using all the mushroom liquid and any remaining broth. The total cooking time should be 25–30 minutes. The rice is cooked when it is "al dente," or tender to bite.

Stir in the seasoning, the remaining butter, and the grated Parmesan cheese. Garnish with the minced parsley and serve immediately, with extra Parmesan. *Serves 4.*

NOTE In Italy, risotto is always served as a first course, but this recipe adapts well as an accompaniment to any broiled meat, duck, or game dish.

Mushroom, Bean & Gruyère Salad

6 ounces thin green beans, trimmed and halved
½ cup fresh or frozen lima beans
½ cup cooked cannellini (white beans)
1 cup sliced button mushrooms
1 cup shredded Gruyère cheese

Dressing
½ cup extra-virgin olive oil
3 tablespoons red wine vinegar
2 teaspoons whole grain mustard
1 tablespoon chopped fresh parsley
Large pinch each salt and freshly ground black pepper

Cook the green beans in boiling, salted water for 3–4 minutes, just until cooked. Refresh in cold water and drain. Cook the lima beans in the same manner, just until tender.

Mix the beans and the mushrooms, then mix in the cheese gently but thoroughly, so the shreds don't clump.

To make the dressing, whisk together all the ingredients until creamy. Pour over the salad and toss gently. *Serves 4.*

NOTE Any variety of cooked legumes can be used in place of the cannellini — garbanzo beans, pinto beans, lentils, or red beans.

Potato & Mushroom Gratin

1 small onion, minced
⅓ cup minced fresh parsley
1 cup shredded Gruyère cheese
2 cloves garlic, crushed or minced
1¾ cups crème fraîche
1 teaspoon salt and ½ teaspoon freshly ground black pepper
2 pounds thin-skinned potatoes, peeled and thinly sliced
12 ounces brown cap mushrooms, trimmed and sliced

*P*reheat the oven to 400°F. Grease a gratin or other shallow ovenproof baking dish.

Mix the onion, parsley, ¾ cup of the Gruyère cheese, the garlic, crème fraîche, and seasoning.

To assemble the gratin, make alternate layers starting with the potatoes, then the mushrooms, spooning the cream mixture between each layer. Finish with a layer of potatoes, laying them in neat, overlapping slices. Sprinkle with the remaining cheese. Bake for 45 minutes to 1 hour, until the gratin is golden brown and bubbling. *Serves 4.*

NOTE For a more luxurious version, use fresh porcini in place of the brown cap mushrooms.

Lima Beans with Mushrooms & Bacon

2 cups fresh or frozen lima beans
8 slices bacon
1 pound button mushrooms, halved
½ teaspoon each salt and freshly ground black pepper
2 tablespoons chopped fresh chives

Cook the lima beans in boiling, salted water to cover for 7–8 minutes. Drain and refresh in cold water.

Cut the bacon crosswise into strips. Heat a skillet, add the bacon, and cook until crisp. Drain all but 2 tablespoons fat. Stir in the mushrooms and continue to cook, stirring, for about 2 minutes. Add the lima beans and the seasoning, and continue to cook for 2 minutes more, until heated through. Transfer to a serving dish and sprinkle with the chives. *Serves 4.*

NOTE This dish is good served with broiled meats. If the lima beans are very large, it's worth peeling them after the initial cooking as the skins can be tough.

ACCOMPANIMENTS

Rich Mushroom Sauce

2 tablespoons butter
1 small onion, minced
1 cup sliced mushrooms, such as
    open cup, brown cap, or wild
4 tablespoons all-purpose flour
²/₃ cup chicken broth

²/₃ cup crème fraîche
1 teaspoon lemon juice
1 tablespoon Madeira
½ teaspoon each salt and freshly
    ground black pepper

Melt the butter in a skillet over low heat. Add the onion and cook until soft, but not browned. Add the mushrooms, raise the heat, and sauté until beginning to turn brown.

Sprinkle in the flour and stir well. Cook for 1 minute, then gradually add the broth, stirring, until smooth and thickened. Add the crème fraîche and stir again until combined. Bring to a boil, then reduce heat and simmer for 3 minutes.

Add the lemon juice, Madeira, and seasoning. *Serves 4.*

NOTE Serve with chicken, fish, eggs, or any broiled or barbecued meat.

Mushroom, Olive & Chili Sauce

Black Olive Paste

1 cup black niçoise olives

2 anchovy fillets in oil

1 tablespoon drained capers

1 tablespoon olive oil

*½ teaspoon Italian herb seasoning or ¼ teaspoon each
dry marjoram and dry thyme*

3 tablespoons olive oil

1½ cups minced brown cap mushrooms

1 clove garlic, crushed or minced

¼ cup chopped fresh parsley

4 tablespoons butter

½ teaspoon crushed red pepper flakes

Pinch each salt and freshly ground black pepper

⅓ cup mascarpone cheese

To make the olive paste, put the olives, anchovies, capers, oil, and herb seasoning in a food processor. Pulse about 5 times, until blended but coarse.

Heat the oil in a small skillet. Add the mushrooms and cook over medium heat for 3–4 minutes, until most of the liquid has evaporated. Add the garlic, ½ cup of the Black Olive Paste, and the parsley and stir until blended. Set aside. (The remaining Black Olive Paste can be stored, airtight, in the refrigerator.)

In a separate pan, melt the butter, then add the red pepper flakes and cook for a few seconds to release the flavor. Add the mushroom mixture and seasoning. Cook for 5 minutes more, then stir in the mascarpone. *Serves 4.*

NOTE This sauce is good with any ribbon pasta. For a smoother sauce, purée before adding the mascarpone.

Savory Mushroom & Cheese Muffins

3 tablespoons butter
1 cup minced open cup mushrooms
2 cups all-purpose flour
2½ teaspoons baking powder
½ cup plus 2 tablespoons freshly grated Parmesan cheese
1 cup buttermilk
1 egg

Preheat the oven to 400°F. Grease a 12-cup muffin pan (or use paper baking liners); set aside. Melt the butter in a medium skillet over medium heat. Add the mushrooms and cook, stirring occasionally, until the moisture evaporates. Remove from heat and set aside.

In a large bowl, mix the flour, baking powder, and ½ cup Parmesan until well combined. In a small bowl, beat the buttermilk with the egg. Add the egg mixture and the mushroom mixture to the flour, blending with a spoon just until moistened. The batter should be lumpy.

Fill each prepared muffin cup three-quarters full with batter. Sprinkle tops with the remaining 2 tablespoons Parmesan. Bake for 20–25 minutes, or until browned and the tops spring back when gently pressed in centers. Transfer to a wire rack to cool. *Makes 10 muffins.*

NOTE These muffins are a delicious accompaniment to any vegetable soup. They're perfect for picnics too.

Mushroom, Nut & Herb Bread

1 ounce dried porcini mushrooms
1 cup warm water
7 cups white bread flour
2 teaspoons salt
3 tablespoons walnut oil
1 envelope (¼ ounce) active dry yeast
½ cup walnuts, chopped
½ medium red onion, minced
1 teaspoon dried thyme

Soak the porcini mushrooms in the water for 30 minutes. Drain, reserving the liquid. Rinse the mushrooms thoroughly. Strain the liquid through a paper coffee filter or a piece of cheesecloth to remove any grit. Add enough warm water to the mushroom liquid to make 2 cups.

In a large bowl, mix the flour and salt. Stir in the walnut oil, then the yeast. Pour in enough of the mushroom liquid to make a firm dough. Knead on a floured surface for about 5 minutes, until smooth and elastic. Return to the bowl, cover, and let rise in a warm place for about 1 hour, until doubled in size.

Chop the soaked porcini finely. Knead the dough again for 2 minutes, then add the porcini, walnuts, onion, and thyme. Knead these ingredients into the dough for about 5 minutes. Shape into 1 large loaf or 2 smaller ones and place on a baking sheet. Cover and let rise again in a warm place until doubled in size (15–20 minutes).

Preheat the oven to 375°F. Bake the loaves for about 30 minutes for a large one, or about 25 minutes for the smaller ones. The bread should sound hollow when tapped on the bottom. *Makes 1 large or 2 small loaves.*

NOTE The dough also can be made into small rolls; brush with beaten egg yolk and sprinkle with a little coarse salt before baking. This bread makes a delicious sandwich filled with sharp Cheddar cheese and some crispy lettuce leaves.

Steamed Spiced Mushrooms in Paper Packets

2 tablespoons unsweetened shredded coconut
1 clove garlic, crushed or minced
3 tablespoons lime juice
1 small red Thai chile, seeded and thinly sliced
½ teaspoon anchovy paste
¼ teaspoon chili powder
¼ teaspoon salt
½ pound small button mushrooms, trimmed and wiped
1 lime, thinly sliced

*M*ix the coconut, garlic, lime juice, chile, anchovy paste, chili powder, and the salt in a bowl until well blended.

Preheat the oven to 350°F. Toss the mushrooms in the coconut mixture. Cut four pieces of parchment paper into circles about 9 inches in diameter. Divide the mushroom mixture among the four paper circles and arrange the lime slices on top. To seal each packet, fold the parchment over, forming a semicircle. Beginning at one end, fold about ½ inch of the curved edge closed; continue sealing, making small folds along edge, until entire curve is sealed. Place the parcels on a baking sheet and bake for 25–30 minutes. Serve straight from the packets. *Serves 4.*

Marinated Mushrooms

¾ pound button mushrooms

4 cornichons or baby dill pickles

½ cup kalamata or niçoise olives

⅔ cup olive oil

Juice of 1 lemon

½ teaspoon crushed red pepper
   flakes

½ teaspoon dried thyme

1 clove garlic, crushed or minced

½ teaspoon each salt and freshly
   ground black pepper

3 tablespoons minced fresh parsley

1 small red Thai chile, seeded
   and thinly sliced

*T*rim the mushrooms. Cut the pickles into thick diagonal slices. If desired, pit the olives. Put all three ingredients in a mixing bowl.

Beat together the olive oil, lemon juice, red pepper flakes, thyme, garlic, and seasoning. Pour the mixture over the mushrooms and mix well. Stir in the parsley. Cover and marinate in the refrigerator overnight. Serve at room temperature, garnished with the chile slices. *Serves 4.*

Index

Chèvre, Mushroom & Walnut Tart 34
Chicken with Oyster Mushrooms & Lemon 27
Chinese Mushroom & Cellophane Noodle Salad 22

Duck, Mushroom & Black Bean Stir-fry 30

Eggplant, Mushroom & Tofu Brochettes 32

Grilled Polenta with Wild Mushrooms & Taleggio 14

Hot & Sour Mushroom Soup 25

Lima Beans with Mushrooms & Bacon 54
Little Fila Mushrooms 18

Marinated Mushrooms 63
Mixed Grain & Mushroom Pilaf 48
Mixed Mushroom Tempura 21
Mushroom, Bean & Gruyère Salad 52
Mushroom & Chicken Terrine 16
Mushroom-flavored Tagliatelle 46
Mushroom Gnocchi 44
Mushroom, Nut & Herb Bread 60

Mushroom, Olive & Chili Sauce 56
Mushroom Omelet 26
Mushroom Pâté 24
Mushroom Ragoût with Toasted Brioche 20
Mushroom, Red Onion & Sun-dried Tomato Pizzas 38

Potato & Mushroom Gratin 53

Rich Mushroom Sauce 55
Risotto with Porcini 50
Roast Fillet of Beef with Wild Mushrooms 28

Savory Mushroom & Cheese Muffins 58
Spiced Mushrooms, Smoked Mussels & Spinach with Couscous 40
Spicy Bean, Mushroom & Chorizo Stew 36
Steamed Spiced Mushrooms in Paper Packets 62

Tuna Steaks with Porcini, Baby Onions & Potatoes 42

Wild Mushroom Soup with Parmesan Croûtons 12